The Saints of Repetition

The Saints of Repetition

poems

Marjorie Stelmach

GRAYSON BOOKS
West Hartford, Connecticut
graysonbooks.com

Again, and always, for Dan

Contents

Another Rainy Night in the World   11

As the Story Goes

As the Story Goes   15
The Director's Cut   16
Sisyphus Reinvents the Wheelbarrow   18
The Magician's Assistant   20
Everything Meant Only Itself   22
Still Life in Progress   24
After the Arts Council Meeting   26
Walking After Dark   29
Lot's Lighthouse   31
The Chord   35
Shakespeare's Death Day   37
The Art of Leaving   39
Door to the River   40

Half-Lives

The Winter Dead   43
Jesus Loved Us   44
Childish Things   46
The Lesson   49
Gingko Leaves   51
The Half-Life of Facts   53
Burying the Moon   55
Dress Rehearsal   57
White Christmas   59
Time and the Rain   60
How It Begins   62

Just Passing Through

Just Passing Through   65

Ivory Black   66
The Saints of Repetition   68
At the Easement's Edge   70
What Matters   72
As the Waters Start Rising   73
Countless   75
You Must Change Your Life   78
The Guesthouse   82
The Easement   84
Let Burn   85

Acknowledgments   93
About the Author   95

Another Rainy Night in the World

Why, on this night of shiver and hunch, are so many
        trudging these rivery streets of small cafés

and darkened shops, all of us hugging ourselves
        for warmth, watching our feet crush

neon sheets into tides that turn the pavement stones
        to a liquid museum of stained-glass scenes

that break like waves on grates and curbs, then re-cohere
        until it seems that under the unrelenting pour,

we, too, might dissolve, again and again, and yet,
        be redeemed by the steady spill that laves

our flesh and jewels our shoes—reminding us
        (we have always known) that we are the poor

who are always with us—though tonight we are
        ravishing, drenched in riches?

As the Story Goes

As the Story Goes

to achieve a long life and a peaceful death,
walk inland until the oar on your shoulder

becomes, not an oar, but a winnowing fan.
Only then will you understand that your lifetime

of steering is over. You've no choice left
but to acquiesce, allow yourself to be tossed

to the winds where what happens next
is not yours to determine. Your fall will seem

to take an eternity, during which time
you'll begin to discern that what you discern

no longer concerns you, and whatever god
you always believed was yours to appease,

that task is complete, your purpose
achieved. Even now—
                              as your story goes.

The Director's Cut

The original was black and white—
improv, for the most part—
and the Garden was a soundstage.
                      We were young,
just starting out, overeager, underfunded.
No costumes, no extras,
       and just the one prop:
an apple,
slick with prohibition.

The sequel's more ambitious.
An epic: cast of billions.
                   We're way over budget:
special effects, multiple locations,
and writers by the score
adding comic interludes,
         flashbacks, chase scenes.

Word has it there's a doozy of a denouement
and dozens, maybe hundreds,
of alternate endings:
         The hero bites the bullet. Or the dust.
Drinks the hemlock. Takes the hill
single-handed. Gets the girl
pregnant.

We've been at it awhile now,
but according to the rumors, this director
takes forever.
           Then there's post-production,
where they say the odds are good
he'll cut our finest scenes.
       But, whatever. It's a part.
We dream of a glittering opening night.
Universal acclaim. Worldwide distribution.
If all goes as promised,
        who knows where this could lead?

Of course, at this stage, it's all speculation.
Anything could happen,
                        it could all go to hell.
But for now, it's a living,
there's an adequate per diem,
                and as long as it's endurable,
we might as well
endure it.

Sisyphus Reinvents the Wheelbarrow

with a nod to W.C. Williams

Rubble, shards of glass, the worn remains
of worldly goods—my wheelbarrow's
overfilled and hard to hold to this uphill track
with only the torque of my shoulders and hips
to resist the tip and collapse,
the spill.

Still, it's a nifty invention. It worked like a dream
for a good long time when the Earth was flat.
But now there are slippery slopes to trod
and a greater dark to navigate—stars
in retreat, mere asterisks left
to light the path.

It only gets worse as I near the peak where
physics itself begins to fail, pop-up infinities
tucked in the folds of the ten dimensions—
or is it eleven—and all our variables
unverifiable. Nothing's the same
as the good old days.

This barrow's become a bitch to keep upright—
teetering, tottering, battered by forces
from the whims of solar winds
to the erratic quirks of quarks.
If my aching back doesn't do me in,
I'll likely die of the tedium, lugging

my assigned portion of the ten thousand things
and all these abstractions: undeserved hurts,
insufficient love, the dust of dreams.
The whole enterprise is growing
old. But the barrow itself?
As beautiful as ever—

capacity and vector in a single machine.
One to a customer and built to last.
No, it's the world that's out of whack;
the higher I climb, the worse the wobble
and the more I need to watch
my step.

But always, at the rim of the great abyss,
the vastness of it takes my breath.
You'd think I'd grow immune to it,
but it's always the same: I lose
my grip, and my haul goes
cascading over the edge.

What, I ask, is the point of this? Why not
just quit? But I know I won't. I'll steer
my barrow back down the slope,
telling myself I mustn't lose heart,
when so much depends
upon
the next load.

The Magician's Assistant

          is a lovely thing, shimmering in laced
costuming, legs netted nearly to the waist.
          An ocean creature, she floats in waves
of gracefulness, each gesture designed to divert
          our eyes from the polished cheat
we came to see—and back again, too late.
          Her role: to see that no one thinks.

She lifts from his shoulders the requisite
          black cape and swirls its scarlet lining
in the lights. He flourishes his tall black hat
          and bows. The show begins.
With barely a pause, she takes from his hands
          lit candles, paper flowers, silks,
linked rings. Their hands touch and part, catch
          and flash. Doves flutter from hollows
in the air. Pockets bloom eggs, eggs hatch
          bouquets and butterflies. Her hands
are gifts of misdirection, allowing *his*
          to slip duplicities into our blinks.

For the grand finale, caped and masked,
          he brandishes swords, thrusting them
into the cabinet she has bowed and smiled
          her way inside. We hold our breath.
When the door opens, a figure emerges—
          whole, unharmed—but something
is wrong. Is it *he* who steps forth from
          the dark interior? How *can* it be?
The figure bows, but no one applauds
          until a second black figure appears
from the upstage shadows: twin magicians?

          Swathed in identical hooded capes,
they spin across the stage, streaming
          crimson ribbons, partners in a daring,
double-daring crime. But which is which?

Abruptly, one throws back her hood,
and her hair cascades in golden light,
        as she unspools a swirling dance
across the stage, pauses, bows, and disappears
        into the wings. Centerstage,
he stills, and silence falls again. He bows
        once, deeply, from the waist,
and suddenly we' re standing, cheering,
        all of us. He is a miracle, this man!
But so is she. The proof? Not one of us
        is thinking *blades* or *blood*.
We're thinking only: *mastery*.

Everything Meant Only Itself

Only madmen and mystics
live without metaphors. —Patrick Harpur

Once upon a time, a hermit rented a hut in the woods.
He thought it might be nice to learn the birds, the stars,
    relearn the seasons.
Or failing that, to find out what it means to be alone.

He found he liked the small hermetic tasks he set himself,
keeping house, keeping silence, keeping sane.
                      On solitary rambles,
he took the woodland trails, but he wasn't a thief,
he always returned them—
    circling the lake, un-circling it.

He began to feel safe: no snakes to his knowledge
(or else very quick). No knowledge, either.
               Everything meant only itself.
Hunting season came and went. He was game;
he stuck it out.

Winter followed: cabin fever, loneliness.
Soon, he was pacing, cursing squirrels, casting them
into outer darkness.
    When they kept coming back,
he praised their persistence.

Spring came around. And summer.
Then autumn again.
Time, he knew, to return to the world.
         The world, he found,
had done well in his absence.
He praised its persistence.

———

The key to exegesis is the *I*—with its iffy implications
         of integrity or irony.

In the absence of an *I*, or if the *I*
is unreliable,
      the reader must discover for herself
what holds *true*.
A golden bowl? a chalice? cupped hands?
          the chambers of the heart?
Something must hold *true*.
God?
        God, it's said, *can use a stone*
as easily as a saint.
Does this make God a Mason?
        a mystic? a madman?
Or just another metaphor?

———

Once upon a time, I listened for the sound
of one God clapping:
        I heard nothing.
I was young. Now, I'm old.
These days, all I hear is my own voice
      praising my persistence.
I no longer need to find out what it means
to be alone.

Still Life in Progress

His studio holds what you'd expect, years of clutter:
      paint tubes, rags, sketchbooks and such;

the stinging smell of solvents; a wide fall of light
      onto an easel where a still life is in progress.

The painting is traditional—a plain wooden table
      draped in white cloth, a loaf of bread

on a pewter plate, a knife, a bowl of plums, a crystal
      water pitcher, and, because he's known

as a master of refraction, an empty glass of light.
      When he returns, he'll fill the glass with water,

forcing light to overflow and wash across the table.
      He hopes that, in the finished work, this light

      will spill forever.

Which leads me to believe he has in mind an allegory.
      Why, then, no dead fish, you ask? No pheasant?

It's true, tradition calls for death, but isn't death
      implicit in this genre's very name?

Resurrection, likewise, and for *that* there's spring.
      Just outside the window (did I mention

there's a window?) birds have flocked to a feeder,
      daffodils shiver in April's chill wind.

And of course, he has included the usual spring mud—
      thick red clay, the worst kind for a gardener.

For a grave-digger, too, should one be needed.
      On the wall beside the window, he plans

to add a painting, a van Gogh, he's thinking,
       but as to which, he's not yet sure.

Perhaps, *Sower with Setting Sun*? Or the famous
       pair of empty shoes? At the moment,

he's leaning toward *A Wind-Beaten Tree*, a work
       stolen years ago and missing to this day.

He's drawn to its torqued beauty. Myself, I'd choose
       that wheat field lashed by winds and

harrowed by crows. They say van Gogh completed it
       just days before he died. Apocryphal, most likely,

but wouldn't it be perfect: a landscape on the knife-
       edge of promise and peril? Not unlike

this still life on the easel—outcome undetermined,
       choices to be made. Unseen forces

       eternally spilling.

After the Arts Council Meeting

A bone-colored day-moon is riding the sky
        above I-70, passing its palm-shaped blessing
equally over the Shrine of Our Lady of Sorrows
        and the exit ramp to Defiance.

Just ahead, another billboard for *Lambert's Café,*
        Home of Throwed Rolls. On it, a man
with a Buddha belly rubs it like a lamp,
        having feasted to his heart's content.

Contentment. Is that what my heart hungers for?
        On a long uphill grade, I pass a Coleman
Camping Gear truck. It passes me back
        on the downward slope, and we do it again

for grins. I imagine him a modern Diogenes
        moving down highways hauling a truckload
of lanterns, still searching for an honest man.
        When he takes the off-ramp to Jonesburg,

he pulls the horn, and I lift a hand goodbye
        before turning my eyes back to the moon—
an honest *woman* with a long night ahead.
        With daylight savings time newly over

and Earth wrenched back on track for winter,
        it's not dark yet, but the moon's hard at work—
clearly a Stoic. Myself, I'll be glad to see this day
        over, the Arts Council quarreling as always

over the state of the arts in the state of Missouri.
        It's all about money. Never enough.
The Seven Lively Arts on life support again.
        What were they exactly? And why

always seven—seven deadly sins, seven sorrows
        of Mary, the seven hills of Rome? I learned

such lists in grade school, back when I thought
        someone would ask, that the world was a test.

Diogenes, too, is still lodged in my head, though
        as cynics go now, he's an amateur. He was,
I recall, a man of some courage, ordering
        Alexander the Great to *Get out of my light.*

He and the moon might have made a good match.
        Have we forgotten who we are?
This is hill country. History here is the story of stills
        hidden deep in the Ozark Mountains,

along with the bones of the hell those boys raised
        in the moonshine days. All of them gone now,
their crimes paved over with concrete and greed
        and all-you-can-eat throwed rolls.

But it's still Missouri—Jesse James country,
        where staying a step ahead of the law is an Art.
Even today, the Lewis and Clark is rife with larceny:
        tourist traps stocked by our local craftsmen

and women, adept as ever at harvesting honey, twisting
        the necks of cornhusk dolls, slicing the bases
of walnut bowls, quilting, carving, and chugging back
        brew, holding their breath as they squeeze off

the shot—you know, the Seven Deadly Arts.
        If my people's blood ran true in me, I'd be
out seeking the seventh son of a seventh son, a man
        like my grandfather, nothing up his sleeve

but history—no Art to that. Time tosses off history
        as nimbly as it paints sunsets on velvet hills,
casts the bones and wins every time, drops us all
        with one shot. Do I sound like a Cynic? I'm not.

That's a philosophy I've no wish to master, not even
        on the night before the test. At last: my exit.

The stars above St. Louis look younger than themselves,
    a trick of time they've been performing

for only a split second short of forever. As for
      the moon, crafty old woman, she's quilting
clouds and casting shadows with a mastery
     that seems, at least to me, entirely artless.

Walking After Dark

Orion strides the sky tonight. Planes cross
     his heart's blank slate at oblique angles.

Below, I mull the darknesses I know best, my own
     and the seventeen-year darkness of my son.

Setting off after supper to walk the neighborhood,
     we head in opposite directions, careful to keep

our paths from crossing. How long ago they seem,
     those nights when my son would grip one finger

of my hand, head tipped back, eyes wide, the universe
     a lake in which he knew he would drown

without me. The dipper spilled its blessings down,
     and all my stories were true. Now, I am a liar,

and he, too. We look lies at each other over dinner,
     carry our separate truths out under the stars.

Ah, Orion. Once, you were my hero. Both of us young,
     remember? You, sword in belt and stride

of a frontiersman, making tracks for the next galaxy
     with your heeled dog. Me, lying on my lawn

holding the words *Milky Way* in my mouth
     like a poem, dreaming immortal lovers

and awakenings larger than lovers, whole cities
     at my heels and you above me, wise and strong,

back when wisdom and strength were one and belonged
     to men. Your heroic stance seems foolish now.

I know men like you. Such men fathered us all,
   untethered men so scattered, so distant from

themselves, not even a faithful dog would follow
   so hollow a creature. These days, unequal

to the sweep of stars, my poems aspire to less,
   confining themselves to simple words,

evening, neighborhood, home, words suited
   to a zodiac dimmed by the glare of cities

and scaled to the strides of lesser heroes. My son's city.
   My boy, who has nothing to say to me

when he comes in. Who goes to his room. *Home,*
   for now, is still the place where both of us

return each night and where my son has learned
   new ways to take me in. After dark,

he'll pace his room, straining against the leash
   of bloodlines and the confines of his heart.

But I sense his stride is growing. Soon, above me,
   silence will fall. He'll stand unmoving behind

his locked door, pondering what it is that sends me
   walking after dark, and what it is he's waiting for.

Lot's Lighthouse

I.
As she sets out across the Great Salt Flats, the encircling
        foothills ripple in the heat like the muscles

of a beast. They are farther than she knows, though
        she knows they are farther than they look.

It's otherworldly, this expanse of white silence,
        cushioned by the soft crush of crystals underfoot.

She has walked the surface of a sphere all her life,
        but today is the first time she has seen it.

Out of habit, she begins counting her steps, liking
        how numbers unfold of their own accord

and drop away unnoticed. She pauses only once,
        to lift a dragonfly husk from the glittering salt.

By what lethal error has it found its way here
        where nothing favors the living? Crystals

sheathe its legs and wings—a metamorphosis-
        in-progress. Beautiful, this alien salt-creature.

Even so, she lets it fall back onto the salt,
        aligning herself with the forces of death,

desiccation, the distributing wind.

She's been walking now for over an hour, and the hills
        are no closer. She glances behind her. No tracks.

No surprise. It would take an axe to mar this surface.
        Thirty thousand acres of salt: a terrifying number.

But the stab of panic at her heart is brief. According to
        her guidebook, people died out here in frontier days,

but no one dies here now. Land speed records are broken.
        Teenagers in jeeps spin doughnuts, shoot at bottles,

test remote-control cars. Strange, then, how all day,
        she hasn't seen a soul. But it's late August now,

and soon, heavy rains will come to flood the plains;
        tourist season is drawing to a close. Regardless,

the emptiness unsettles her. Turning back, she chooses
        a number at random and resumes her counting.

She hasn't the heart to start over.

II.
A well-known sculptor has come this summer
to work on the famous Bonneville Flats.

He has worked in bronze, wood, glass, and stone,
but recently he's grown aware of damages

done to the earth in the name of art, and he knows
        he must choose a new medium—Time.

Each finished piece is a singular briefness, carved
        from eternity and returned to the earth.

At dawn, he loads his rented van with gallon water jugs,
        paints and sketchbooks, cameras, blades and axes.

Then, he drives onto the flats to chop from the salt
        his signature shape, the one imprinted on his cards

and catalogues: a tall, narrow house with a steeply peaked
        roof—the kind a child might draw. After years,

its clean lines and simple proportions are still pleasing
        to his eye. He will title this current piece

Lot's Lighthouse.

Working on the flats has not been easy—unrelenting
        heat, intractable salt, eyes stinging from sweat

and refracted sun, long hours alone. His back and arms
        ache, and he worries he will lack the strength

to hoist the salt house upright—a slab of salt
        this size is exceedingly heavy, and he is

no longer young. But, if all goes well, the photos
        he will take at sundown will provide

a striking poster for his next solo show—
        a white tower rising from a vast white plane

stretching away toward Earth's white edge: white
        on white on white, awash in the shades

of one day's dying.

If he can't complete his work before the rains begin,
        he will let the piece stay horizontal,

shapeshifting metaphorically from house to boat.
        Or to coffin. From *shelter* to *rescue vessel*

to *casket*. He smiles at this foolishness. If the worst
        should occur, he'll just change the name.

What matters is to finish before a shallow lake begins
        lapping at its base, returning it, sooner

than planned, to its elements. He shoulders his axe
    and re-finds his rhythm, each stroke chipping

shards of light from the horizontal sun. But now,
    for no reason, he is picturing dragons, *white*

dragons wheeling above wide and darkening waters
    at Earth's verge—guardians of an ancient world

returning to its elements.

III.
When she sees the first gleam in the distance,
    she is sure there have been others before it,

a steady rhythm of glint and gone. She quickens
    her step. (Just after dark, the rains will begin.

If the sculptor lowers his axe, she will be lost. But these
    are truths she knows nothing of.) How strange

this life, she thinks, where a thousand miles from home,
    she finds herself walking a plane of salt, guided by

a pulse of struck fire from a source unknown. The hills
    at her back take on the shades of smoldering coals,

but somewhere out there at the visible edge of Earth,
    a human shape is carving light. She begins

to count the flares like blessings.

The Chord

Early evening in a light spring rain a young composer
strolls the gravel roadway leading to his studio.

He'll work into the night layering bits of world-sound
beneath a nearly finished score—a fabric of shadow-tones

moving in the depths to roughen the surface. Maybe
he will borrow the rumble of the eight-fifteen as it sweeps

beneath the overpass sounding its hollowed major sixth.
Or maybe the lowing of cattle turning homeward.

Or the nearly inaudible B-flat sputter of the overhead wires
that, hours from now, will seem in the darkness

immeasurably louder. At the fence he gazes off
across the field to where three horses stand shivering

in the rain. As evening takes the last of their shadows
from the grasses, he pulls the caul of his rain jacket

tighter to his throat.

What is it he hears inside that cloth hollow, this quiet
composer who works in a syntax of frequencies and rests,

who has strained all his life to hear the pitch of the planet's
workings? Listen: is he humming? Summoning

the horses? Enticing them to drift a little closer to the fence,
to stand with him awhile, shifting a bit, as creatures will,

breathing softly, as he tunes his thoughts to his night's work.
When he extends his hand, they step forward and begin

eating music from his palm, the gentle movement of their lips
an intermezzo he will carry to his studio, where it may serve

the work. Or not.

They stand together at the fence: three horses curried
by silver rains; a young composer sifting through

Earth's offerings to find a phrase or cadence so enduring
it will weave itself into a perfect counter-grain.

Perhaps tonight he'll find a way
to score the quivering haunches of the storm.

Above him, clouds rush eastward toward the hills,
the horses merge into a shadowy trinity

and move away.

Night's begun the long caesura that absolves us all,
dissolving the scene so flawlessly it may be true,

or not, that the earnest young composer, after looking
skyward one last time, lowers a shadowy baton

and returns it to the world—a grave and decorous
gesture, in response to which, like any accomplished soloist,

the world bows in return.

Shakespeare's Death Day

A day like this, perhaps—dappled sun, dew globes
glistening in the grasses; insects at their business

lifting wire-thin bodies, fleet and indistinct;
a solitary cardinal, man of many calls, splashing bright

against the vines that twine the fence wires.
The dead of the intervening centuries are legion,

but those of us still here—the quick, the dying—
mark the date. What, I wonder, would he think?

Spring's ruin is scattered everywhere you look,
lightning-scarred limbs, stark against a screen

of leaf buds, gaps in the hedges, patches of bare dirt
splotching the lawn: a drab and damaged scene.

All of it random—no apologies, no blame—
only Earth, editing her deathless prose toward truth.

To me, it seems fitting that on this day the world
take note—proof that, in the over and over

of earthly lives, a single narrative might still rise
from the muddle of our telling—a life to catch an arc

and ride the centuries. Though mostly our stories
sink back unremarked into the mesh and hush of history.

I'll spend this morning celebrating in my fashion, bingeing
on the glut of quotes that flood my email feeds and blogs.

I'm glad for all the fuss, but first, it's nice to stand
in my doorway and snag my eyes on a solitary wasp,

faithful little wisp of stem, wing and compound eye,
one of nature's underlings patrolling a humble plot,

hoping for a sip of nectar or the chance to lug back
to its young a corpse exuding a tangy edge of rot—

but finding mostly scarcity. Impressive, the courage
required this day of the least of us. And tomorrow

and tomorrow and tomorrow. Shakespeare
might have deemed this wasp a hero, facing up

to what the world decrees, never asking if its fate
is in its stars. Or in itself. Or, like the rest of us,

still in doubt. Some questions last the centuries—
one more gift, on this day of his death, to celebrate.

The Art of Leaving

i. Excavation site, Cerén, El Salvador:

What they found in the settled ash:

fourteen-hundred-year-old beans,
fragments of thatch, a tethered duck,
teeth tossed onto the roof for luck.

Nothing decomposed: supper table,
coals, a cooking pot, four emptied bowls,
bedrolls not that evening unrolled.

In one bowl, narrow ridges chart
the path his fingers swept—the man,
who, leaving all he owned, fled

with a life fourteen centuries gone.

ii. A grotto in Southwest France

What they found in the cavern's dark:

two fourteen-thousand-year-old dents
formed by the knees of the artist who worked
a charcoal bison into the wall,

the simple strokes his fingers left
in the softened clay, his barefoot tracks.
There remained no trace

of an overlaid print—it seems
he chose to work alone—until, one day,
his work complete, he reentered

the light and never came back.

Door to the River

after the painting by Willem de Kooning

Imagine a door. Now, remove the attachments—
the hinges and knobs—extract the word *wooden*

like a splinter from your heel, and there you have it:
wide open, all yours. Pretend you're Huck Finn

fleeing Pap's shack, lighting out for the river.
There, on the bank, mud-footed as an otter,

simply slip through the surface. See? Not a ripple.
You *can* swim, can't you? If not, or if you fear

the cold, or if you've been told the currents here
are treacherous, you'll find a raft half-hidden

in the tall river grasses. It's sturdy, river-worthy.
Like shavings of sunlight afloat on the water,

this raft can never sink. Climb aboard, push off.
As the day heats up, ease into the cool. The river

will hold you like a hammock roped at one end
to the ocean, at the other, to the upstream sky.

Lean back. Close your eyes. What you hear
is the purl of a paddlewheel lifting

slices of water and setting them down again
as softly as time's passing. And yes, time *is* passing.

Soon you'll be leaving, but don't be concerned,
the leaving is easy. Imagine a doorway.

Now, remove your attachments . . .

Half-Lives

The Winter Dead

Clothed in shades of shadow-
        on-snow, the dead
take up their watch among
        the winter trees and begin
in the lowering sun to elongate
        toward tomorrow.

They had wanted to last.
        They still want to last,
want it harder each day
        of their absence.
And we want it, too.
        But less and less.

Only their vestments
        betray time's passing,
paling from bone to linen
        to parchment. In time,
they'll sift into the tangle
        of the understory,

and it will become our part
        to keep watch
over the easement until
        our grief has lessened.
Then we may rest, although
        there will be days

we still sense their presence,
        settling like last light
into that hidden place
        close to the heart,
where we store our own
        future ashes.

Jesus Loved Us

Our father was driving. Our mother's hand
would lift into dashboard light to touch
his forearm or shoulder. He'd turn to her and smile.
When he raised his eyes to the mirror,
we'd seem to be sleeping.
                           Do you remember it, too,
those suppers with family friends across town?
How, after we helped clear the table, we'd curl
into Afghan-draped rockers or the corners
of sofas, half-hearing the shifting of ice cubes
dissolving in tall glasses.
                           Soon, we'd drift off
in a lull of voices that filled the evening
around us with names we half-recognized
and stories we knew were somehow our own.
Later, we'd wave to the shadowy forms
on the porch and climb into the backseat
where silence settled around us.
                           Leaning back
we'd look up through the side windows,
letting the shadows wash over our faces.
Streetlights, trees, and stars streaked away,
and ahead, the dark opened all the way home
down the streets of South City—Elm,
Oleander, Potomac, Arbor.
                           One of us would start
singing, and together we'd move through
our quietest songs, the ones we sang only
on nights like those: *Puff the Magic Dragon,*
I See the Moon and the Moon Sees Me,
Jesus Loves Me.
                           Back home, in our bedroom,
Jesus the Shepherd waited on his hillside
to fade away slowly above our prayers
into a darkness broken by the gentle,
intermittent passing of headlights
on the far wall.

                        We slept well
in those days, remember? We dreamed,
I suppose. Morning came. This was
before everything changed. Anyone
would have loved us then.
It wasn't hard.

Childish Things

People like us who believe in physics know
that the distinction between past, present and future
is only a stubbornly persistent illusion. —Albert Einstein

She watches from the dock as future rainstorms
lift in sheets of mist, leaving on the lake's skin

the horizontal ghosts of trees. In school, she'd learned
that every rain is part of a single world-rain

that rises and falls and rises again: it's called
the water cycle—one of the patterns that govern

Earth's workings. There are others. If she watches
she'll find them. She's been keeping watch all summer.

Every afternoon, she sees the trees' reflections reaching
toward the far shore, and every day their reaching

comes to darkness. Another cycle. Sadder. Just now,
she's watching her water-face rippling, ghost-thin,

at the dock's end. Last year in science, she learned
the human body is mostly made of water. It's odd

how science is meant to make things clearer,
but just as often it only shows that everything's

more hidden than you thought. Today, she misses
her earlier world. When she was little, time passed,

and she never even noticed. Now, summer is almost
gone. Soon, she'll peel her reflection from the lake

and head home. Last summer, her mother's face
rocked gently next to hers in these waters. This year,

the only face is hers, as if this year she must be both
herself and her mother's ghost. Another odd thought.

She knows these are *her* thoughts, but sometimes
they appear out of nowhere, forming and passing

like clouds. Another thing: this summer, more
of her thoughts are memories, maybe because

she's older now, and thoughts are made partly of time.
But time is made of nothing. Not even atoms.

If time were to pass above the lake (as, of course, it is),
it would cast no reflection. Still, everybody knows

time exists: *today, next year, last summer*. Last summer,
they were all here together, but over last winter

there must have been a day when *last summer* changed
and, to her mother, it meant something else.

Something sadder. Now, it means something sadder
to her, too. She knows if you think long enough

about a word, its meaning changes. Or the world
changes around it. Or it's you that changes.

People say *everything changes in time*, so maybe
we aren't mostly water. Maybe we're mostly time.

Or mostly thoughts? She wonders what became
of her mother's thoughts, after? Did they lift like mist

to join an immense cycle of world-thoughts?
If that were true (she knows it isn't) they'd come

back around, and one day she'd wake remembering
her mother's memories. Except, she would *be*

one of those memories, wouldn't she? Another
odd thought. She lets it go. Time does move

in cycles, though. Days of the week, seasons of the year.
Maybe that's the reason people believe in ghosts.

Ghosts aren't scientific but, just for a moment,
she lets herself believe that, like mists that rise

into the water cycle, someone who you know is gone
might not be. Or maybe, not forever. If so, might that

explain why these memories have come to her? Maybe
they have come from her mother, come to help her

keep the watch.

The Lesson

The day they came to live at the lake house,
Pepper vanished, and Salt turned hunter—

birds and small mammals eviscerated
on the slab out back or splayed on the dock

for Chi to come upon at first light:
Dad, look what Salt's done!

Chi leans in and stills his breath to take in
the lesson spread for his six-year-old eyes—

anatomy, yes, but there's more to this.
Something about empathy, necessity,

morality. About the world's complexity.
This, anyway, is what his father hopes.

Gradually, Salt's trophies become
merely another of the lake house stories,

and no one asks that Salt comply with rules
that aren't Salt's own. In time, it's okay

to skip the shoe-box burials, to squat instead
beside the remains, mapping the architecture

of flesh, the paths blood takes, the way bones
link and break, make cages for the heart

and brain. Or to walk past inattentive, letting
the blood stains ease away in the next storm.

It no longer feels wrong to take what seems
worth keeping—feathers, bones, whole wings—

to add to his box of Special Things alongside
the key to a wind-up rabbit, sea shells,

pinecones, his shorn baby-braid. It's all
so interesting, this world. Some of it

you save, turning it over in your hands
before prayers. Some of it you leave

to the use of others or the work of the open.
The long trick is learning which is which.

This, at least, is what his father hopes,
though after this spring, his father

will not be here to see it.

Gingko Leaves

Again, this year,
it happened overnight—
the communal letting go. Now,
for a single week between seasons,
I'll walk the paths of Forest Park
through mounds of gold.

Today, they're spread
like softened honey over the hillsides,
a trove of autumn's coins newly minted.
A few will lift in the breeze like grace notes,
as if to touch a final time the emptied
staffs above them.

Tomorrow, I'll find them
swirling downslope like young dancers,
all limbs and gymnastics. Down by the lake,
a flock of geese buried to their bellies
in treasure will rise resplendent—the geese,
the leaves—to scatter gold light
on the waters.

On days three and four,
they'll laze in November's thinning sun,
slug-a-beds, a bit worse for the weathering,
sated and spiritless, edges beginning
to brittle in the cold.

But, if we're lucky,
they'll linger through days five and six
to shed a radiance over the low hills
and lawns—a last muted glory before,
at dusk, their gleam succumbs
to winter's stars.

　　　　　　　Heading home tonight,
I'll slow my steps; every year,
these liminal days come and pass
too swiftly. Behind lit windows,
children are dressing in costumes of
fluorescent bone. Hallowe'en
was my mother's birthday. Tonight
will be hard.

　　　　　　　But tomorrow,
on All Saints Day, I'll move with throngs
of my city's faithful on the sidewalks
outside the cathedral. As we pass
one another, deep in our privacies,
each, in our own way, visiting graves,
we'll exhale soft halos—
a white-gold currency. Coins
for the ferry.

The Half-Life of Facts

There are formulas now for the half-life of facts—
how long it will take in a field of knowledge
for half of what we know
                                to be wrong.
In medicine it's fifty years. Seven for psychology.
Engineering, maybe three.
                        For math, far longer. Infinity?
It started with gauging the age of rocks.
Then, elements and isotopes.
Uranium made the concept famous:
                                704 million years.
                    (It's the *four* that knocks me out.)
Now, post-docs spend their scholarship years
in underground labs bent to their screens,
computing the half-life
                        of everything
and publishing papers that perish
almost at once.
        All this, to prove
that we grow obsolete over time,
not wise—a fact, I suspect,
with a long half-life.

Mostly, I'm okay with it.
But a few years back, scientists found
                    that ants can pass the mirror test.
Those tiny paragons of group-think can gaze into
a laboratory mirror and,
        like toddlers and chimps, recognize themselves.
        Their *singular* selves.
Looking back now on my anthill-trampling youth,
I'm ashamed at how heedlessly I passed
the half-life
            of my moral code.

In her final years,
my stepmother moved to the Memory Wing,

gradually losing our names
                    and finally, her own.
Who *was* it, then, staring back from the mirror
of her numbered room?
              Some days, she knew.
But more and more often,
she wasn't sure.

Down the hall in the Memory Wing
lived an elderly woman who wanted to die.
                         As she steered her chair
through the corridors, she begged everyone
whose face was familiar
              to help her go,
and we, as instructed, told her gently
she didn't mean it,
           reminding her
how much she was loved,
how badly her family would miss her.

Those who study such things assured us
her wish would lose its urgency
and drift away in time.
                But who she would *be*
when that time came,
no one could say.
         Already, I'm told,
we've begun to learn
that our knowledge of dementia
                         is mostly wrong,
leaving me here in the Memory Wing,
long past my half-life and
                    knowing less
with every day—only enough
to be afraid.

Burying the Moon

        Knowing
how hunger links to cold,
my backyard squirrels
scurry to the burying.
In their world of thievery
and tactic,
every acorn counts.
        But winter
is a two-edged sword,
and Earth might be
a kinder place if squirrels
could grasp the principle
of unintended consequence—
how a small lapse of memory
can beget an oak.

        This awful year
I sat with you, as story
after story slipped the edges
of your memory. Haltingly
you offered them to me
before they disappeared
for good.
        One day,
a secret kept for decades
and intended, I'm sure,
to be taken to the grave,
passed instead into
my keeping,
and everything I knew
tipped and slid.

        No matter,
that I never asked to know.
No matter, that you didn't mean
to speak. Now, I'm part of it,
and technically,

I've held my tongue—
except . . . this poem.
    And worse,
these dreams. Nighttime,
shadows of a thousand oaks
and layers of drenched
October leaves, in which
I must bury
moon after moon, until
I've buried ours.

    Grief alone
is hard enough.
Harder,
not to know the whole
of what is asked of me
or what, one day,
will come of this.
    It was from you
I learned how surely
silence links to love.
This winter's task: to find
how best to bury
the past—and carry
one more silence
to the grave.

Dress Rehearsal

Tonight, no one calls them by their household names.
Tonight, they're sheep, a camel, a donkey.

In the Great Hall, the pianist practices E minor scales
on an ancient upright. When she lifts her hands

you can hear the scratch and yap of manger beasts,
exiled to the parking lot. Backstage,

there's a whiff of rancor left over from casting,
a lingering scorn on the lips of the simpering angels,

a feud brewing between the kings and the shepherds.
But these are the final days, all roles assigned,

all assignments past change.

For a congregation, it's a perilous season—
friendship and ego locked in their standard wrestle,

parental pride, as always, a treacherous presence,
illness in the cast a grim likelihood, and nothing

to be done about the weather but toss another handful
of salt on the sinister glisten of the sidewalks.

The elders, who live all year in E minor, herd
the chorus into line. Lights dim. The mothers

are breathless, as if this were opening night at the Met.
Each child holds a burning candle, a timeworn device—

the simple fact of bearing fire will sober even
the rowdiest child. As they pace forward, a soft light

laps the sweet under-flesh of their jaws and everyone
present is caught in something unnamable. Call it

the *Fear of the Lord*, an antique sensation of which
we are all in denial. To prove it, we join our voices

in Advent's desolate hymn: *O Come, O Come...*

Apparently, he will come from above. We lift our eyes
to a gold star hung from the rafters. From below,

no one sees the bent points or the patches of glitter
rubbed raw on the long ray that points to the stable.

Ah, we think, they're so young. Too young, perhaps,
to be exposed in this holy season to a minor key

that, from this year forward, will obscurely
wound them. This is the annual silent accounting.

We all feel it: fear of what will come in the long year
ahead. None of us knows who will be called upon

to pay, though the cost is no secret to the elders,
who are, nonetheless, bravely applauding.

White Christmas

Just at dusk the snow begins,
small lights countering
        the planet's darkening.
Ahead, a long night
of gradual erasure.

Out there, it's an etching:
black limbs nailed to a pewter sky,
        snowfall lifting lamp posts
into ghostly suspension.
Gauze stretched

to cover a hatch-work
of wounds. Tell me once more
        why we choose
for the child to come
over and over again like this.

What counterweight
could ever serve
        against the centuries
ahead—so much darkness,
such cold?

Time and the Rain

Outside, the wind churns the bushes and rattles the screen.
Inside, the child on the playroom floor is stringing wooden beads

into a necklace. As she works, she is learning to link the sound
of rain to the warmth of her room and both to the nameless

rush of blood that deliciously shivers her skin. Her work
is only beginning: she is tuning her heart to the purl of time.

Already she knows how to thread the moment just over
to the one to come. Soon will begin the harder work

of aligning the visible world with the one that vibrates
behind it unseen. The child is young. The world is stern.

The rain bears down.

The old woman's room looks over the courtyard, its window
wide to the springtime rain. The sill is soaked, but her eyes

are weak and she doesn't notice. She finds the rain's song
soothing. Especially now, when she is so often alone.

This morning, she pages through photo albums searching
for faces that match her memories, turning face after face

to the light, then folding them back into the dark. Some days,
she's sure there has been a mistake, that these books belong

to someone else. Someone old. Most days, she knows
this is not the case and she must try harder. From the courtyard,

she hears the hum of machines at work on the hedges and lawns,
the steady purr of ongoing industry—such a safe sound.

Or maybe it's raining.

Beads lie scattered on the playroom floor. The child has tired
of playing. Each bead requires her full attention—it isn't easy,

so many shapes and colors, though their holes are identical
empty circles. *Time* is teaching the child-stringing-beads

how to construct her one life. Of course, mistakes will occur,
so the child must learn, too, the difficult art of forgiving herself

for the future.

The old woman dozes over a book of someone's past.
The child has completed her necklace. Soon, it will be

naptime. Both the child and the woman will wake
into a world washed clean of faces.

For a few soft moments, this will not be frightening.
Then, it will be frightening again. Both will call out.

One mother will answer.

In her room overlooking the courtyard, the woman hears
the last of the raindrops falling into a growing silence.

The sound is easeful. It seems to have come from
a long way off—a place that contains a necklace of beads,

rain song, her mother's voice. She knows she is gradually
losing the thread of her past, but she smiles to herself.

Her time here on Earth has taught her the world
is forgiving. She knows this world will forgive her

for going.

How It Begins

It will come to you wrapped in the soft cerements
                                of the after-dark rains.

It will enter your awareness like the memory
                        of a long-ago companion.

Still, you will not wish to go.

You'll be given time to grow accustomed.
                                At first, you'll resist,

speaking more and more often in the future tense,
                but soon, you'll tire of such complexities

and wish for a stillness in which to make ready.

Please be assured that all will be accomplished
                                with immense care

and your body, old companion,
                will be there to lead you,

having always known the way.

Just Passing Through

Just Passing Through

On average, African elephants weigh
twelve thousand pounds.

Clouds weigh a hundred times as much.

Clouds, too, travel in majestic herds,
as they have for four and a half billion years—

though their names are a mere two centuries old:

> *stratus, cirrus, cumulus,*
> *translucidus, velum* . . . and on and on.

For eons before our coming, their shadows
passed namelessly over the Earth.

Imagine the weight of that silence.

Time is a difficult language to master.

Some days, it's good to remind myself
that all of Earth's most precious creatures—

elephants, clouds, words, eons—
are just passing through.

Some days, it's only another wound.

Ivory Black

A common black. Transparent.
Much valued by painters.
Lightfast: resistant to fading.

Once, it was made from cast-off tusks—
gathered, charred, and ground to a powder.
Now, the tube reads: *Unspecified bones.*

Elephants in the wild, it's said, will carry
the bones of their dead for days,
the whole herd slowing to the pace of burden.

They pause for a time at the burial site,
to perform what rites seem needful.
It's believed that they mourn.

Elephants are imperiled now. Each year,
20,000 are shot by poachers who harvest
the tusks for black market profits,

their carcasses simply left to decay.
But you knew this, right? With a mere
eight tusks, a man can advance from

marauder to millionaire overnight.
Elephants, now, have begun to evolve
at a desperate rate, genes

for tusklessness passed to the young,
half of whom will be born unequipped
to survive in the wild. But then,

the world changes, doesn't it?
It's best, don't you think, to accept it?
Losses like these are really

no more than the cost of living.
Here. On Earth.
Where nothing is *lightfast*.

The Saints of Repetition

The rain has finally stopped . . .
it hurts to be alive, but only with a distant ache.
—Fernando Pessoa, *The Book of Disquiet*

I've been watching a pair of bluebirds
            ferrying straws past my window,
coming and going, ignoring the raindrops—
little saints of repetition.
            It's been one of those daylong rains,
puddling the sidewalks, soaking the lawns,
sinking into the rail-bed gravel, lingering
over the churchyard
            to darken the headstones—
a rain falling equally on travelers and graves.

All morning, the soft burr of rain-song has run
on continuous replay,
            summoning a world at the far edge of memory:

            The rain is raining all around,
            It falls on field and tree,

            It rains on the umbrellas here,
            And on the ships at sea.

So much of this world is set on continuous replay.
No wonder, sometimes, we grow weary.

Weary: a long acquiescence of a word.

            Come unto me, all you who are weary
            and heavy laden . . .

                        Well, aren't we all?

Even the rain must grow weary—
all those circular journeys over oceans and mountains.
Over eons.

And stars: for three thousand years,
we 've followed a cycle of heroes and beasts
across the night sky, their glorious stories
dissolving in their wake.
Meanwhile, the heavens keep on expanding,
dismembering legends,
their component stars racing full tilt
toward the edge of the universe
clutching our fate in their fists.
By now, they're so distant
that, gazing straight at them,
we can't be sure they exist.

As above, so below:
down here, we hurtle through time,
as if desperate to know the end of our story,
when the truth is
we know it already—a lightless universe
of travelers and graves.
And all of us weary:
the woman hurrying past with the huge umbrella,
the drenched dog-walker, the Fed-Ex man,
the ships at sea, the heavy-laden,
my industrious bluebirds, and those like me,
who stand at a window watching it rain:
we also serve
no purpose.
Only continuous replay:
gathering what straws we can gather
to build what nests we can build
in what time we have left,
while the rain keeps falling—
equally, as promised—
on us all.

At the Easement's Edge

Late afternoon. A lassitude drifts over lawns and back porches, stillness hovers in the slackening light, and the air above the trees is inked with omens. It's in these unassigned hours that all the day's doings come gradually undone.

At the easement's edge, I make out a small mounded shape like a newly closed grave. A bird? One of the mourning doves I've been watching all week, cooing and preening out on the deck rail? Shadows begin to pile up around it. It may or may not be a dove. May or may not be dead. I turn away without knowing.

For every living creature—human, vole, or dove—a breath will come that will be the last, and, in the moments after, it begins, the unraveling. The body's cogs loosen. Flesh flattens and frays. Tissues thin to entropy.

Given the choice, who would not choose to vanish into that final breath, the way our burdensome flesh disappears into dreams?

My recurring dream: I am standing at an upstairs window, gazing down into the easement. Below in the moonlight, my shadow scatters my ashes.

After a night of unsettling dreams, I wake expecting that transfigurations have been worked in my absence. No surprise, then, to find there's *nothing* this morning at the edge of the easement. No trace of a dove. Or a dove's remains. Or some creature that never was a dove. *Nothing.* Not even the ashes of an absence.

I fear for my eyes, for all they have built in my lifetime on the unsteady scaffold of light.

Hypothesis: The World Tree of myth is a drill, grinding unceasingly deeper, snarling Earth's fault lines, wringing her rivers dry, tangling the lives of the dead irreversibly. This would explain why I wake some days to diminishing echoes of a *dies irae*.

We should hone our vigilance, all of us, for what lies ahead. Not that it will matter.

There's a Blood Moon predicted tonight, which is why, in the wee hours of morning, I'm out on my deck looking up. Spread over the sky where the full moon should blaze, there's a flannel cloud-cover vaguely backlit. Another spectacular lunar eclipse I'm asked to take on faith.

In years past, the Leonid meteor showers have proven just as ungiving. Still, there are those who have gone to the trouble of charting the skies for millennia. The least I can do is to gather my paltry wishes, appear as instructed, and honor our annual scatter of stones. Like visiting graves.

You'd think I'd learn, but, come August, I'll be out here again at the easement's edge watching the sky, as another night-watch comes to naught. It's hard not to hold a grudge.

Still, should a night finally come when the heavens surprise me with clarity, I'll have my wish ready: that the ancient inscrutable Man be erased one night from the full moon's disk by the scythe of our synchronized blink of indifference. Let him live in the dark for a time, as we do.

What Matters

*The weights of all things must be
determined anew.* —Nietzsche

Ferguson, August. Leaves like a million gavels suspended
above city streets where night after night protesters gather

with cardboard posters, limp from our famous humidity.
Hand-lettered slogans, hastily written, letters more crowded

    as they near the right margin.

I'm not in that crowd. I'm at home watching last night's
footage. I need to rethink things. My city. Myself.

The self I still hear regaling my students with tales
of my own days of protest—impassioned demonstrations

    I thought would change everything.

Then for decades, I let the marches go on without me
while I wrote poems, endlessly tinkering, working

toward perfection: title, point of view, pacing, line breaks.
Read your poems aloud, I urged my students.

    Listen to every vowel, every consonant.

Steer your reader toward meaning with stresses
and pauses. Vehemence, reticence. Every line

must be cut to exacting measure. Pay close attention.
Each choice matters. Not only your words.

    Every last breath.

As the Waters Start Rising

All things by immortal power, near or far,
hiddenly, to each other linked are,
that thou canst not stir a flower,
without troubling of a star. —Francis Thompson

When the hundred-year floods swamped
Australia's bushland, thousands
      of ground-dwelling spiders
cast silken threads into the air,
sheeting the land with a seamless,
                    diaphanous webbing.
The video took my breath: mile on mile
of shimmering billows spread out over
      farm fields and grasslands,
lifting a legion of eight-legged exiles
to safety.

At our best, I believe, we're a lot like
those spiders. Say, a child falls into a well,
      or miners are trapped
in collapsed mineshafts, or a soccer team
finds itself in a cave as the waters
             start rising.
Word passes swiftly, and soon
the whole world is following updates,
         riding the waves
of risk and rescue, spinning out tissues
of thoughts and prayers.

Watching those spider-throngs' triumph
lifted my heart—but only as long
      as the video lasted.
Then, atavistic, my horror clicked in.
I confess, every spring
            I broom
Cottony balls of spiderlings down
from high corners—somebody's infants.
      I murder them all,

proving, for me, a spider's a spider,
no matter how small.

What's a human to do with the baggage
of being a human? For some, it's bats
          come to tangle our hair
and suck blood. Or snakes winding silent
in dust, smiling a toothless malice.
                    We're hardwired:
these creatures are coming for *us*.
And yes, I know, this world is not about me.
          It's about what's ahead
(or not) for us all. For warblers and scorpions,
microbes, chickweed, flounder and fawns.

Even spiders.
Doubtless, spiders are eons further along
          on that ancient journey for which
we keep spinning our own DNA. Those waves
of translucent silk studded with spiders
                    agleam in the sun,
sharing a life raft crafted and spun
from their very essence—they make for
          enthralling viewing.
But my heart won't have it.
How long, O Lord, how long must we wait

to evolve a gene for *agape*?
Some days, it's a comfort to know
          your mercy endureth forever.
But, *ours*? Not so much.
Still, maybe one day, we'll watch a flock
                    of our better angels
go viral across the web, and we'll want
with all our hearts to join in, start again.
                    And maybe
it won't be too late by then. But I think
it will need to be soon.

Countless

after the Flammarion Engraving

In the list of the *countlessnesses* we humans construct
        our hyperboles on, sand always comes first,

its grainy shiftlessness shifting beneath us or sifting
        listlessly through our fingers, its protean gifts

enabling us to build our elaborate sandcastles, only
        to watch them fall to the tides. Stars are next,

innumerably strewn through our oldest tales—and
        more innumerable now in our lenses.

Third, the myriad lives lived on Earth and the earth
        those lives decay into before taking on

the next shape they'll briefly assume on their eons-long
        trek down the mix-and-match, shed-and shine

paths of even the most modest atom. But me? I knew
        I had only one life in which to complete the task

I'd set as a child of counting from one to infinity, vying
        in endless games of one-upmanship, each of us

trying to prove that *my* "huge" is huger than *thine*.
        In time, I developed the all-encompassing

sense of mission required for impossible tasks,
        along with the strength to endure the defeat

I'd assuredly fall to. Meanwhile, the concept
        of *countlessness* changed. The 20th century

turned our single *infinity* plural—*infinities* now
        enfolding and intersecting each other, dooming

our best equations, consigning our finest hypotheses
        to the dust. (Dust: yet another *countlessness*.)

And so, I gave up, dropping math like a match held
        too long in my fingers, and took up *Love*.

I found the two have a lot in common—pain, for one.
        Like a singed marshmallow, love proved

sticky, sweet, and searing, clogging my breathing and
        tearing my eyes. Love drove me mad.

Madnesses, too, we know now, are legion. Consider
        the genius, Georg Cantor, who, in the aftermath

of his infamous trespass, crossing from the realm
        of the countless into the Countless,

was driven mad by infinity's endless cascade
        of integers sieving through space-time.

Waking from his technicolor dream into
        the plain black & white of the world,

he found himself in a padded cell. What he felt,
        I suspect, was incalculable loss.

Picture that famous engraving: a sorcerer down
        on his knees, derrière in the air, head

thrusting out from beneath our own starry
        canopy into a star-crazed firmament.

It's clear from his posture that, quick as a photon,
        he ducked back under his local sky,

counting his blessings, content with his life-sized
        life, gladly leaving immensities to

those angels dancing so fast on their pinheads,
　　　　they blur into—what? The all-encompassing

One, that primary prime we're taught to call
　　　　Love with a capital *L*? Or into the cosmic

Zero, the nothing-at-all we all started from?
　　　　Whatever. Such things are beyond me.

I have this one life. It's going fast. From the start,
　　　　it was always a countdown.

You Must Change Your Life

Our times:

Our times, they say, are uncertain,
as all times are, I guess.

> But it seems to me
> that what our times
>   are uncertain of
> is us.

> > *Faith and physics:*
> > > *The natural density of a Higgs boson*
> > > *is* zero.

> > God Particles are, for many of us,
> > a difficult camel to swallow.
> > >   How enormous, then,
> > is a mustard seed
> > in this new, enigmatic
> > >   scheme of things!

Ancient wisdom:

The oracle instructs us:
>   *Know thyself.*

But, having discovered
that every cell of our body
>   is a changeling,
shouldn't we choose a simpler wisdom
to live our lives by?

Gothic cathedrals:

In centuries past, children learned young
to stand in the cold
                    and sing.
I can't decide if that was a good thing.

Angels:

Look it up.
          You'll find *angel*
          between
anachronism
and *atheist*—

with the rest of us.

The cost:

Longing is not without its costs.

Moonlight is laced with the dust
of dead moths.

The sadness of van Gogh:
          . . . but what's the use.
                    —last words in van Gogh's
                    final letter to his brother, 1890

It's the missing question mark
that breaks my heart.

Kindness:

Everyone is carrying a burden.
Or so we're told
by those who urge us to be kind.

Fatuous, I think (unkindly).

But this week I learned our atmosphere
weighs 5000 trillion tons.

True stories:

For years,
when asked about my childhood
I'd say: *My mother died*
          when I was very young.
Now, I say: *My mother died*
               very young.

It has taken me nearly
the whole of my life
          to hear the difference.

In the Memory Wing:
The truth is that nothing changes anything
and what we say or do only brushes
the tops of the mountains in whose valleys
all things sleep. —Fernando Pessoa

So it is,
I brush my stepmother's hair.

Weary:

Some days it seems too much to ask
that we suffer the scuff
                            of life's
continual asking.

At the graveside:

Only as the graveside service begins,
do I understand that
                    Let us pray
is a plea.

The Guesthouse

A house of high windows, commodious views,
      lawns sloping down to fields of tall grasses.

Inside: flocked wallpapers, inglenooks, cornices,
      hearths we've been warned are too old for use,

and above in the guestrooms, a time-polished silence.
      From downtown, a train whistle enters

the ambience, sounding so low in its throat
      that I hear it as sobbing. Say that I found it,

the word for this ache—*rueful, autumnal*—
      of what earthly use would it be?

———

Who knows what they use for bait in the mousetraps
      they've stashed in the kitchen, but if you're

the first down to breakfast and find a small corpse,
      the house rules dictate it's yours to dispose of.

Yesterday's mouse, half-way in / half-way out
      of its cardboard coffin, was so tightly gripped

by some hidden device, when I pinched its tail
      and pulled hard, I felt only resistance.

In the end, I pitched the box, mouse and all,
      into the trash, but I carried the force of

that grip in my head for hours. Whatever it died for
      last night in the dark, I hope it was sweet.

———

Out where the trash bin releases a smell of small death
      and vegetable rot, there's a half-open gate

to the prairie. A smoke-odor hangs over the trails from
        last week's controlled burn, aborted for safety

when gusts rose mid-day. The team will be back, though,
        with chemicals, spray guns, and fireproof suits.

Hubris, I think. But what do I know about prairie fires
        or the management of the slow burn? My place here

is only a room in a guesthouse. My time here is short,
        almost over. And my dead, as is right, are mine

to dispose of—house rules I've only just learned on the eve
        of departure. For the time remaining, it seems

that what's mine is to work on the wording. A breeze
        sweeps over, bending the grasses, pausing, passing.

I hear it as laughter.

The Easement

A flock of purple finches perches
      eye level in the easement trees,
all of them itching, pecking incessantly,
      probing their feathers, tossing
their heads, shrugging their wings,
      to eject what nits and grit
they can reach—not enough, it seems,
      to relieve their torment:
what riles them has burrowed in.

      I call this my meditation time,
but mostly I'm sifting the daily debris:
      my badgering past, our political
rancor, the fires and floods that threaten
      our heartland, our coastlines,
our streets, and war, always war—
      the churn of my own inner silt
that won't settle these days.

      But these *birds*. Little scoops
of immense concentration, abundant
      of flutter and scant of flesh,
torquing themselves as if bent on ousting
      life's myriad irritants, knowing
perhaps that this too is their life.
      It's a thing worth knowing.

Let Burn

Most afternoons, I ramble the old logging roads—
deep-rutted trails that break from the highway
                    to enter the woods
and weave through our scatter of glacial lakes
before ending abruptly in tracts
                    of impassable brambles.
It's official now, this drought. With every step,
I crush a crisp pine-needle sheet—a tinder sound
as unnerving
            as cracked knuckles.
One more reminder of my weight on Earth.

Let burn: policy of the DNR,
established late last century when fires blackened
                        thousands of acres of hardwood.
This evening's *Daily Mining Gazette* confirms
that conditions are ripe this year
for a conflagration.
                        At the state park entrance,
they've posted a schedule of *controlled burns*—
a homeopathic cure
                for sweeping destruction.
To me, it sounds like madness.

So little has changed here: the same nameless mix
of fungus, ferns, and fallen trees
                    we stumbled through as kids.
Mine was a nurtured ignorance, resistant
to shelves of field guides
            and elders who knew the whole world by name.
I tell myself, I was raised in a landscaped world.
I tell myself, we learn what we need.

As if that were an answer.

———

If you drive the peninsula's one highway north

toward Copper Harbor, you dead-end at Lake Superior,
largest freshwater lake in the world.
                It's a longer drive than I remember,
dotted with signs of a generational poverty:
boarded-up stores, closed schools,
rusting trucks kept for parts,
          and ramshackle houses: FOR SALE.
I spot a few recent additions: American flags,
Trump signs, a newly built prison, and, chained
to mailboxes along the highway,
              jet skis and ATVs
hung with homemade signs reading:
Make me an offer.

Between towns, I drive through patches
of scorched forest, spiky charred trunks upright
                   on an earth etched by fire.
And by fire's aftermath: wild flowers.
I search out the names in my grandfather's field guides:
        chickweed's pale petals, low to the ground,
fireweed's magenta, spires of deep blue lupine,
and a gush of devil's paintbrush,
             flashing a stagey red-orange
as brazen as Scratch's beard.

Devil's Paintbrush: a recent addition to Michigan's list
of invasive species.
        Parasitic, the field guide tells me. *In extremity,
it will drink the juice of neighboring roots.*
                  It's our own fault.
Settlers brought it here as an ornamental,
and like so many of our bright ideas, it requires
          a vigilance we don't possess—
or only in *extremity*.

           ——

This year, I'm alone in the cabin.
The evening quiet out on the screened porch
unsettles me.
        Loon calls enter at dusk.

Bats steer their eerie silences through the last of the light.
When the hoots of eastern screech owls
                    begin to scribble the distance,
I'll head indoors.
All night, I'll hear animals move in the dark.
The back screen door
                    will strain at its hook in the wind
and return to its frame with a sinister knocking.

My mother's people have been coming here
for over a hundred years.
                    The North, in those days,
was a harder place: brutal labor, black lung, isolation,
snowfalls two stories deep.
                    Only lantern light flickered along the lakeshore,
backed by the unbroken darkness of dense, unlogged forests.
Help had a long way to travel
                    through endless stretches of nothing.
And reigning over it all, Lake Superior's unfathomed deeps,
unforeseeable storms, unrelenting cold.
                    They must have learned early to take precautions.
Learned, too, that taking precautions
would not be enough, after which,
there was only endurance.

———

I read somewhere that we share with trees
a chemical kinship so close
                    that changing the central atom
of one molecule—magnesium to iron—
will turn chlorophyll
to blood.
                    In extremity, then, could we learn to drink
from each other's roots?

———

Over fifty summers ago, I watched my dad
tie a sturdy rope to the leg of a wrought iron bed,
                    coiling its length beneath.
That year, we practiced lowering ourselves

from the window of the loft, in case of fire.
He tried to make a game of it,
          but our mother had died the previous year.
That summer, I dreamed of Bambi,
of flaming woods and fleeing creatures.
                    At bedtime, Dad would tuck us in
and return to the beach, keeping watch over our campfire
until long after the last coal died.
                    Now that he's gone,
his children and grandchildren take the same precautions,
despite a volunteer fire department, a shoreline ablaze
with electric lights,
          and boats sufficient for our getaway.
But vigilance goes only so far; we know, one day
we'll need to be rescued.

                    ——

Beach fires are forbidden now, signs along the highway
announce, *Fire Danger: HIGH.*
                    Across the lake,
the shoreline goes totally dark as the sun goes down,
but the cabin windows fill with light.
                    I imagine families at Scrabble boards,
quirky letters turning up like oddball cousins,
the youngest children learning
                    the power of blanks,
along with the risk of holding out
for the perfect placement of Z's and X's—
          the way, at game's end, everything you keep
counts against you.

Alone, and unequal to Solitaire,
I drag out the broken cardboard box that holds
our ancient Scrabble set
                    and draw my seven letters—
a token gesture.
I let the cool tiles of the boneyard
slide through my fingers over and over,
                    while the radio casts static
through the aurora borealis—ghosts crossing over

from adjacent stations: newscasts, call-in-shows,
polka music, opera—
                    cryptic messages tangling and flaring,
like the threadbare ribbons
of the northern lights.

After midnight, back on the porch, I rock in the dark
watching the lake lift silver ripples
            that briefly ride the water's black surface
carrying a ghost-light cast by a million stars—
only some of them living.
                                I once thought
my childhood stars would be there forever,
but within my lifetime we've learned that the heavens
are largely empty,
            constructed mostly of entropy and dark matter,
that the stars are picking up speed
in their urgent wish
                    to escape from each other,
that the gorgeous ribbons of the northern lights
are violent solar winds licking our atmosphere
like cold flames—
            no discernable pattern,
            no discernable purpose.
How could such knowing not have changed us?
                    Does anyone still believe it's our task
to watch until the last coal dies?
It requires a vigilance we don't possess.
                                And yet . . .

                    ⸻

I tell myself that Time's cosmic promises
were designed for vastly longer lifespans than our own,
and that one day,
            in the aftermath of some cataclysmic disaster,
a nameless loveliness will blossom
                            unsummoned,
like the one I've watched unfold this summer—
chickweed, lupine, fireweed, devil's paintbrush—
            a litany of benign fire tonguing the Earth.

Let burn:
it still sounds like madness.
But, whispering the words tonight,
                              I hear it begin
to sound like prayer.

Acknowledgments

Acknowledgment and thanks to the editors of the following publications in which the poems listed below first appeared, some in earlier versions or under different titles.

The Anglican Theological Review – "White Christmas"

Boulevard – "Burying the Moon"

Chicago Quarterly Review – "The Chord"

Canary – "The Easement" & "Ivory Black"

Cave Wall – "Shakespeare's Death Day"

The Christian Century – "Another Rainy Night in the World" & "How It Begins"

I-70 – "The Guesthouse" & "The Lesson"

Innisfree – "Time and the Rain"

Lake Effect – "Let Burn"

The Other Journal – "Dress Rehearsal"

Pensive: A Global Journal of Spirituality & the Arts – "Jesus Loved Us"

Presence – "What Matters"

Sand – "Childish Things"

Sisyphus – "As the Story Goes" & "Everything Meant Only Itself"

Slant – "Dress Rehearsal" & "Just Passing Through"

Talking River – "Sisyphus Reinvents the Wheelbarrow"

Third Wednesday – "The Winter Dead"

"The Lesson" is dedicated to my brother, James Herweg (1954-2001).

"Lot's Lighthouse" is dedicated to prominent Bavarian sculptor, Alfred Böschl (1949-2020), whose work is described in this poem.

I have been enriched over the years by the presence in my life of fellow poets Barbara Crooker, Jane O. Wayne, Allison Funk, and Bob Lowes, who served as first readers of these poems, and who generously provided inspiration, encouragement, wise suggestions, much-needed caffeine and the occasional Martini, along with the precious gift of their friendship.

I am indebted to the Virginia Center for the Creative Arts for fellowships that, over a period of nearly thirty-five years, have provided a beautiful setting, the company of amazing artists, and the precious gift of time to concentrate on my poetry. My thanks, as well, to Ragdale where a number of these poems had their beginnings.

My special thanks to Ginny Connors at Grayson Books for offering suggestions that strengthened these poems and for her patience and care in the production of this book. My thanks, too, to Cindy Stewart for her fine cover design and careful copy-editing.

Finally, to my dearest Dan, my on-going thanks and love.

About the Author

Marjorie Stelmach is the author of seven previous volumes of poems, most recently, *Walking the Mist*, 2021 and *The Angel of Absolute Zero*, 2022. A selection of her poems received the first Missouri Biennial Award, and her first book, *Night Drawings*, was awarded the Marianne Moore Prize from Helicon Nine Editions. She served as the first director of the Howard Nemerov Scholarship Program at Washington University in St. Louis.

www.ingramcontent.com/pod-product-compliance
Lightning Source LLC
Chambersburg PA
CBHW070804120626
46557CB00002B/708